# The Craft and Commerce of Video and Motion

New Opportunities in
The Converging World of Still Photography & Motion

**GAIL MOONEY**

ISBN 978-1482544268

Published by Kelly/Mooney Productions
Brookside, NJ USA

Photography © 2010 Gail Mooney
www.gailmooney.com

Photo of Gail Mooney © 2010 Erin Kelly

*For my mother Nola.*
*Who taught me to believe in my dreams.*

# Table of Contents

# Introduction

I was inspired to write this book after receiving countless phone calls and emails from still photographers who had questions about incorporating motion into their businesses. The emails and calls started slowly at first after I began writing a blog entitled, _Journeys of a Hybrid_, which is geared toward still shooters who were moving into motion. When I started giving seminars on the topic of video, I quickly became overwhelmed by the amount of correspondence I was getting. I realized something had to give when I was spending more time talking with photographers and associates about their projects than I was on things that I wanted to do. I also realized after giving countless seminars, teaching and consulting, that there is a hunger for this information so I decided to write this book.

I had already created two ePubs that were compilations of posts from both my professional blog, _Journeys of Hybrid_ and from my film project blog, _Opening Our Eyes_. One would assume that an ePub, made up of previously published blog posts wouldn't sell. I have found that not to be case or at least not my experience. People are quite happy to pay $4.99 for an ePub rather than to have to cull through my blog posts and archive them in book form themselves.

It wasn't until I received an email from someone who had taken one of my seminars that I knew I was on the right track as far as the approach I should take in putting this book together.

They wrote:
" I just wanted to tell you that your seminar was extremely inspirational even though I can't really say I learned anything new. Thank you."

Ten or fifteen years ago I may have taken that as a negative remark, but when I read this note, I actually took it as a huge compliment. More importantly it was a very telling statement. These days we are overwhelmed with information. There is so much free content online, there are some days that I get lost in a sea of information spending enormous amounts of time sifting through it, yet not really feeling like I'm getting anywhere. On top of that there are traditional books, ePubs, podcasts, webinars, seminars, and workshops galore. It's become so easy to disseminate knowledge that we end up with a lot of the same information, just repackaged.

I started to think about the "why" in terms of what people hoped to take away from a seminar or learn from a book.  I believe that most people want to get information that they will be able to apply to their own businesses. Statistically only 2% of workshop participants will act on what they have learned.  Sometimes people feel so overwhelmed by information overload they can't even get started applying the information. Instead they end up giving themselves excuses and reasons not to.  So when I read that comment from someone who had taken my seminar telling me that I had inspired them, I realized that should be the end goal, both for the giver and for the receiver.  I realized that the way to inspire someone to act would be to not just provide them with the same basic knowledge they can get anywhere, but to deliver the information in my own voice and speak to my personal experiences in the business of motion.

The content in this book will cover the fundamental basics of sound business practices in video production, along with real case scenarios from my own business. I have found that by sharing my own experiences it makes it easier for people to apply the information to their own businesses. More importantly, when information is delivered in an authentic and passionate way – it does inspire.

Read on and get inspired.

# 1

# MISTAKES STILL PHOTOGRAPHERS MAKE WHEN MOVING INTO MOTION

It might seem like pointing out mistakes is an odd way to begin a book, but it's better to learn from other people's mistakes than to make them yourself. I have compiled a list of the most common mistakes that most still photographers make when entering the world of motion.

- **They forget about the story.** It's not the camera that tells the story – it's the person using the camera. Pretty visuals slapped into a motion timeline with music don't necessarily tell a story. Video is a story telling medium. Don't forget that.

- **They throw in video clips for free.** One of the best opportunities that still photographers have when expanding their businesses with video is to offer this new service to their existing clients. I hear from so many still photographers who kill this opportunity from the start by throwing in the video clips for free because they are "*still learning*". I'm not a fan of learning on the job. I prefer to hire crewmembers that are good at various skills that I don't possess. More importantly if you give the video away because you're still learning, the question is "At what point will you have learned enough to charge for it?" Who will decide that, you or your client?

- **They think they already know how to shoot.** If you think because you are a professional still photographer that all you need to do is buy a DSLR capable of shooting video, you are mistaken. Shooting motion is far different than shooting still images. An experienced motion shooter can spot video that has been shot by a still photographer who has little "motion" experience, right away.

- **They focus too much on the "tools" and not the technique.** These days video equipment is relatively affordable. Therefore the bar on the entry-level to video production has been lowered. If you don't want to price yourself out of business by positioning yourself as cheap, then be unique and have your own vision or point of view that separates you from the pack. Resist the urge to be all things to all people.

- **They don't collaborate**. Get over the one-man band model by trying to do everything yourself. Video production is a collaborative effort. Surround yourself with a crew of experts that will make you look good. Build a team of editors, sound mixers, motion graphics artists that you can draw upon.

- **They position themselves as DP's or Directors** If you assume the role of a camera operator, a DP or even a director, you will most likely be working in a "work for hire" mode. Instead position yourself as a producer – shoot and direct if you want to – but realize that if this is the sole role you choose to play you'll be just one rung on the content creation ladder.

- **They try to compete in old business model markets**. Everyone aspires to shoot broadcast spots and feature films. They think that after shooting motion for only a few months – or even a year – that they will be able to compete in the high-end market of commercial video production. This market like the still photography market has changed drastically Many times it has been marginalized by still photographers who are just starting to shoot motion and are shooting video jobs for next to nothing because they have no understanding of the business.

- **They treat audio as an afterthought.** Capturing good audio is more important than making a great image. If a viewer cannot understand the dialog they will not watch your video. Don't make audio an afterthought. Hire a good sound person.

- **They forget about the editing and output.** Shooting is one thing – editing it and getting it "out" is another. **Learning to edit will make you a better shooter.** You quickly realize in the editing room what you SHOULD have shot in the field. But it's also important to understand that you can learn from watching an experienced editor. A good editor will raise the bar on your projects. Editing is a craft and an important part of video production.

- **They learn the "how to's" in terms of gear but nothing about the business.** There are hundreds of "how to shoot motion" workshops out there, but no one seems to be teaching "the business" of video production. Still photographers think they already know "the business" but quickly realize they don't, and often put themselves out of the video production business before they've even begun.

- **They are underinsured.** Video production has many variables. Many times that means larger crews and bigger budgets. If something goes wrong on a video shoot and you need to place a claim with your insurance agent who provides coverage for your still photography business, they might pay the claim but drop you as a client. Re-examine your insurance needs.

- **They don't consider the ramifications when working with SAG (union) talent.** Clients may ask you to shoot video of union talent on a still photography job. This crosses the line as far as the unions are concerned. While it may be OK for SAG talent to work on a "still" set, when you go into video mode it's not OK. If I know I will be working with union talent I will hire a casting agent who will act as a signatory and take care of the necessary union mandated bookkeeping as well.

- **They don't license their work.** This is usually not a possibility if you are *just* a shooter and are "working for hire". As a producer, working in a business direct market, I am able to maintain ownership and copyright of not only my content but also the whole production. In addition, I license any "frame grabs" that can be pulled from the footage and used as stills.

- **They don't learn interview skills.** This is what separates the pros from the still shooters who have DSLR cameras and think that's all they need. I'd say about 70% of my work requires me to do on camera interviews. I'm the one who ask the questions but I am not on camera or part of the final edited interview. I need to know how to ask the right questions that will provide stand alone answers in order to produce usable interview clips for an editor. That means knowing how to get great sound bites from my subjects. This is one area I excel in. It's all about my rapport with my subjects.

- **They under-estimate what a job will cost in both time and resources.** There are many facets to video production – the shoot, the sound, editing, music, motion graphics, scripts, voiceovers and delivery. You won't be hands on in all these facets but you'll need to determine these costs and present them in your estimate. This is where experience comes in. If you lack experience in this area, hire a producer.

- **They neglect to draw up a production schedule.** This is essential in project management and for keeping a job on target. Make sure that each step of the project has a delivery date specified with a sign off signature required.

- **They look at video as a separate market.** That's changing rapidly as video is no longer a separate niche or market, but rather part of almost every photography market from editorial to architecture. Even ad agencies are starting to merge their motion and still departments.

# 2

# RECOGNIZING
# NEW OPPORTUNITIES

Many still photographers ask me: "Where are the new opportunities?" They probably expect me to answer this question; by simply saying "video", but video in itself is not a "new" business model, nor is it a "market" per se. Video is used in many markets; fashion, sports, weddings, corporate work, and education. In fact, many photographers moving into motion overlook the new opportunities in video by pursuing the more traditional markets of commercial broadcast work.

My partner and I work in business direct markets. We take the lead on jobs as producers and are responsible for the entire production. We maintain ownership and copyright of the "whole" as well as the individual "assets" we create and we license usage accordingly. Most of our work is created for the "web" and external as well as internal communications. Our business model may not work in the commercial advertising sector because most agencies have separate divisions for motion and stills with a more traditional model in place, but that is quickly changing. The commercial shooters I know who have successfully expanded into motion and are directing broadcast spots, generally have separate representation for their still and motion work.

Initially, it was our still photography clients who began to hire us for their video needs. With the proliferation of mobile devices and a shift from print to electronic delivery in terms of how we communicate, there is an ever-growing demand for video. I caution photographers who are just starting to shoot motion, NOT to throw in the video footage for free if their client asks for it on a still shoot. If you do, you will have already devalued your new "service" or skill set.

If you are thinking of expanding into motion ask yourself these questions first:

- Do you enjoy collaboration?

- If so, what role(s) are you comfortable with on a production team? Producer, Director, DP, Camera Operator or Gaffer? I throw in gaffer because it's a gaffer's job to light the set and many photographers love this part of the craft and are really good at it.

- Can you handle the responsibilities of a producer? The trade-off is that you get control and ownership of the production. If you are used to working this way in still photography, you should realize that the responsibilities are amplified in video productions.

- If you only want to operate the camera then understand it will most likely be a work for hire situation. Can you accept that?

- Will you offer still images **and** video to your clients?

- What markets do you work in now? How will video be a part of that?

There are opportunities everywhere and in every market because video content is not restricted to expensive media buys on broadcast TV. Many small companies and non-profits are finding that not only they can afford to create great videos and push them out via numerous online platforms but they also realize that delivering their message in the video medium is very effective. But technology is a double-edged sword and along with new opportunities comes increased competition as the entry level to video production gets easier and more affordable. Carve out your own niche and style. That way you won't end up competing just on price. That's a quick race to the bottom.

The choices are up to you. How do you see yourself in the world of convergence?

## What Still Photographers Need to Know About Convergence

We should not just think in terms of how we can apply the newest tools of the trade to how we are shooting today, but rather think about how these tools and future versions of them will affect how we will be delivering the message in the years ahead. We should also be cognizant of the fact that it is not the content creators that will be determining the tools of the future, or how and where the content will be delivered, but rather the top executives and bean counters of camera companies, advertising agencies, broadcast networks, movie studios and magazine and newspaper publishers. They will set the stage and the content creators and receivers of the content or the "audience" will react.

These days content creators have numerous options to choose from when selecting the tool or camera for the job– everything from an iPhone to a camera like the RED which is able to produce 5k resolution stills, shooting at 96 frames a second, at a 1/200th of a second. We make our decisions based on a number of factors; affordability for one and determining which camera is the best fit for a particular job. Many times it's the end use that dictates that decision. We should remind ourselves that not only our tools are changing but so is the way that information or content is disseminated as we rapidly move from print to electronic delivery. Simply put, mobile devices have dramatically changed the way consumers are receiving content and information and we must adapt or die.

Who could have imagined just a few years ago that a phone could take photographs that weren't just "good enough" but really good in terms of resolution and delivery? We need to keep in mind that the limitations of today will most likely not be limitations in the future. Technology is changing our lives and our businesses in an exponential way and will continue to do so. If we are smart and want to stay in business we need to be able to look forward and imagine what's next, rather than to look back at what was or be complacent with what is.

When I started my still photography career more than 30 years ago, a professional photographer needed certain technical skills. We needed to be able to focus a camera and that was tough if you were shooting fast moving action subjects. We also needed to know how to get an accurate exposure. The cameras of today have pretty much eliminated the need for those skills with auto focus and auto exposure. Still photographers still need to know how to light something or manipulate existing light but as software becomes more sophisticated will that still be a necessary skill set in the future?

When I give my seminars to still photographers who are thinking of moving into motion I start out by explaining the differences between the two mediums. Still images are "moments in time" and video is "time in motion". That explanation may sound simple but it's quite profound when you think about it in terms of the convergence between these mediums over the last few years. While today's cameras have pretty much eliminated the need for technical skills of knowing how to properly focus and expose an image, a photographer or camera operator still has to be able to *see* and capture the "decisive moment". But going forward will that still be a skill that is necessary with motion cameras able to shoot at 96 frames a second at a fast shutter speed and with a 5K resolution? Why would a client need a photographer to shoot still images when they are able to pull frames from motion footage? Most likely a client won't need a *still* photographer in the future, especially when most camera operators in the motion sector are working under "work for hire" contracts and they don't hold the copyright to their footage and/or the still images or frame grabs that get pulled from that footage. That's a *game changer* for the still photography business and the business model of licensing of images.

I read an interview once with Vincent LaForet where he relayed a story about a discussion he had with a DP at a RED trade show event shortly after the RED One camera came out. He asked the DP, "Who in the world would want to shoot a still image with this huge RED camera with a Cine lens? It's insane. Why wouldn't I go out with my 5D Mark II that shoots RAW?" The DP answered "We want to take your still jobs away from you just like you want to take our video jobs away from us with your HD SLR's."

That was a few years ago.  Now I hear that a lot of high-end commercial still photographers are shooting with smaller, more affordable and higher-resolution motion cameras to shoot their still photography jobs - and so are DP's.  That's convergence. Who knows what the future will bring? One thing is for sure, it's best to be knowledgeable in both mediums and not be complacent with what is.

# 3

# THINKING AND SHOOTING IN MOTION

One of the biggest assumptions that still photographers make when they start shooting motion is that it's no different than shooting still images other than it's a different setting on their DSLR cameras. That couldn't be further from the truth. Shooting motion requires a different way of thinking.

## The Differences Between Still Photography and Video

- A still image is a moment in time.
- Video is time in motion. You should shoot to edit and that means thinking and shooting in sequences, not just shooting isolated moments in time.
- Audio is more important than the video. If your audience can't hear or understand the dialog in your video they'll turn it off.
- Video is a collaborative effort. Still photography is more of an independent pursuit. Build your team and collaborate with people who possess skill sets that you don't have. The best example of this would be to hire a "sound guy" when first starting out. Capturing good sound or audio is not a skill that most still photographers have.
- In video the story is everything. It's not about the *tool* (the camera) – it's about the story. I see so many photographers fail at creating good videos because they lose sight of the story by focusing too much on the gear.

## Using Sequences to Tell the Story

- Shoot scenes as sequences made up of a variety of shots, not just one long run-on shot. It's more interesting visually and you'll be glad you did when you go to edit the piece. Sequences are made up of a variety of shots with various camera angles, focal lengths and points of view. But keep in mind that you'll need to put these shots together in post-production, so when you are shooting always think about how you are going to "get into" and "out of" a shot. Shoot to edit and visualize the "whole" or the end result. Think about what will come before a shot and what will come after a shot. Don't wait until you get into the editing room to figure out how they will juxtapose one another.
- You can use movement to help drive the story sequences. This could be subject movement, camera movement, background movement or all three.

- A director needs to decide whether to use multiple cameras or multiples takes if using only one camera. If you are able control the action and will be using a storyboarded shot list, then you will be able to shoot multiple takes and move the camera around. If you don't have control over the situation like when covering an event, then using multiple cameras positioned at various places will work best.

## Shooting Tips

- Let your subject move into and out of the frame.

- *Crossing the line or the 180 rule* – Imagine your shooting area as a circle. Draw a line down the middle of it cutting the circle into two halves. You can shoot from anywhere within one side of the circle. If you cross over and shoot from the other half of the circle, you've crossed the line visually and the audience gets confused.

- Shoot action/reaction. Example: When shooting a classroom situation, shoot a variety of shots of the teacher, then turn around and get shots of the students reacting.

- Shoot and move. Get a variety of shots from different camera angles and focal lengths. Shoot the same scene getting wide, medium and tight shots.

- Shoot lots of Close-ups. They add interest and drama and play well on small mobile devices. Wide landscape shots that make great prints on a museum wall won't have the same impact when viewed on the screen of a small mobile device.

- Use *motivated moves*. Don't *pan* or *tilt* the camera unless you are using those camera moves it to convey a message to the viewer. For instance, a slow camera move or *tilt* that starts at a basketball player's sneakers and moves to the top of his head, emphasizes the fact that the player is very tall. A pan moves the camera from side to side. A tilt moves the camera from top to bottom or the reverse.

- Don't shoot video like a still photographer. Retrain your trigger finger to hold a shot for 10 seconds or more. Many still photographers either start rolling the camera too late or stop the camera too soon.

- Don't use the auto features of the camera – no auto focus or auto exposure. Remember you are capturing time in motion not a moment in time. Auto focus and auto exposure will change during your shot and the exposure as well as the focus will change as people move into and out of the frame.

# 4

# THE STORY
# IT'S EVERYTHING

No matter which market you choose to work in the "story" will be of the utmost importance. Whether you are producing a 15 second spot for broadcast, shooting a testimonial video for a corporation or making a feature film, the story is everything. The medium of video is perfectly suited for story telling. It utilizes sound and movement in addition to visuals to tell a story and therefore plays to more of our senses. It's a medium that's ideal for evoking emotion. But too many times still photographers make the mistake of concentrating too much on the gear and not enough on the story.

Every story starts out with an idea. Ideas have always come easily to me, usually when I least expect it. All sorts of environments or activities can trigger ideas.

Seth Godin wrote a blog post entitled, "*Where do ideas come from?*" Here are a few of my favorites excerpts from it:
- Ideas come out of the corner of the eye, or in the shower, when we're not trying.
- Ideas come in spurts, until you get frightened. Willie Nelson wrote three of his biggest hits in one week.
- Ideas occur when dissimilar universes collide.
- Ideas fear experts, but they adore a beginner's mind.
- Ideas hate conference rooms, particularly conference rooms where there is a history of criticism, personal attacks or boredom

Once I come up with an idea, I start focusing the story in my head. I play out the movie in my mind. What is the message? Whose message is it – mine? – my client's? What is the motivation or goal of the piece? What is the call to action? Is it to entertain, inform, or ask for donations? What is the end goal? Once I get a clear idea of what the story is about I start to put the pieces together. This not only demands that I come up with answers to the questions that I've outlined above, but also that I identify the intended target audience.

If I'm working on something scripted, then the script needs to be written and a storyboard needs to be drawn up. Then I'll need to cover all the bases in pre-production as far as casting talent, assembling a crew, creating schedules etc.

If I'm working on a documentary I know I won't be working with a script, but I will be starting out with a very clear vision of the story that I'm after. That usually entails a lot of research. After I've fully developed my story and researched it thoroughly I will assemble a crew, identify and schedule my subjects for interviews and plan out what b-roll I will need. (B-roll is explained in the next chapter) The more details I work out in the pre-production part of the process, the better off I'll be in the production as well as the post-production part of the process. Not everything goes according to plan, especially in documentary work. Many times I need to be flexible, but I try to eliminate potential problems before I begin production.

Regardless if I'm working on a scripted piece or a documentary, the edit is the last line of defense in creating the story. As a director I need to make sure that the story I want to tell is told. If I'm doing the editing I'll start by gathering all my assets before I begin. This includes the interviews, b-roll, still photos, music, stock footage, motion graphics, voiceover track etc. If I'm working with an editor I'll try to do a pre-edit and deliver all usable footage, sound recordings, still photos and other content that I've created. It's a lot of work but it forces me to become familiar with the material so that I can be helpful in the post-production process. The editor will take it from there, research and find the appropriate music, graphics or any stock footage or still images that may be necessary. I will either guide the editor on what the story is that I'm after by delivering a written "treatment" or providing a very rough timeline of my content, preferably using the same software application that he or she will be working with.

For example when I was in post-production with *Opening Our Eyes*, a feature length documentary, I went through all of my footage first. Then I selected the best interview sound bites and laid them down in a timeline sequence in Final Cut Pro, my editing software application. This not only gave my editor a very clear idea of the story I wanted to tell, but it kept my costs down because I was doing the grunt work of transcoding footage and sorting out the chaff. It also allowed me to become familiar with my footage so I could make suggestions when working with my editor. This particular documentary was made up of nine different stories of people on six continents who were making a positive difference in the world. The stories were unified by the theme "the power of the individual" or "the global power of one". That was my unifying theme from the moment of concept to final post-production. Whenever I got tempted to add something to the mix that didn't belong, all I had to do was ask myself if it was aligned with the theme and would drive the story where it needed to go.

So, how do you tell the story? For me, it's focusing on the idea at all times and editing toward that purpose. There are hundreds of ways to tell the same story, but you need to know what the story is before you can begin to tell it.

# 5

# THE FACETS OF VIDEO PRODUCTION

**Interviews** ("A" Roll) Many times your interviews will drive your narrative or your script. This is especially true in documentary work and often true in corporate work. Getting great interviews is a skill set but is also dependent on having a good rapport with your subjects. The interviewer should be the "people person" on your team who will make your subject relaxed and want to talk. A good interviewer is also a good listener.

**B-Roll** The visuals that will illustrate what the interview subjects are talking about. It is also used to illustrate what a narrator is talking about. B-roll provides relief and interest from seeing "talking heads" on the screen. For example if a subject is talking about how much she loves to ride horses, then the b-roll will be footage of her riding a horse. Make sure you shoot plenty of b-roll. You can never shoot too much.

**Live Action** This is footage where the visual and the audio are captured together. For example if I were to shoot a teacher instructing her class, I would shoot with the idea that I will be using both the audio and the visual from the same footage. I need to make sure that I capture good sound as well as a good picture in the same footage. This is different than using the audio captured from an interview with the teacher and using b-roll of her in the classroom for the visual.

**Audio** The most important element of all. Whether you are recording an interview, a voiceover narrative or ambient sounds your audio recording must be clean and be able to be heard and understood by your audience. Hire a sound person if this is not in your comfort zone.

**Script/Narrative** This can drive the entire piece as in a fictional movie or can be part of a piece like a documentary where it is used to tie all the other elements together. A good script can make or break a movie. Even the best actors look weak if they are given a bad script.

**Music** Imagine a film or a commercial without music. Music adds feeling and emotion. It also drives the pace and rhythm of a piece. It is integral to the whole and sets the mood.

**Graphics/Motion Graphics** Some pieces rely heavily on graphics. Look at some of the graphics that TV networks use or shows geared to children. They can be very complex or quite simple like white text on a black background. I usually outsource complex motion graphics.

**Still Images** Ken Burns uses tons of still images in his historical projects. Leave time for research if you know you will be relying on still images. You can make still images come alive by making them move in the edit part of the process.

**Editing or Post-Production** They say that editing is the last line of defense for the story. You can edit the same material different ways to tell a hundred different stories. I have the utmost respect for what a good editor brings to a project. It's where all the elements of your video come together.

**Output** The number one question you should ask your client is "What is your end goal or deliverable?" Many times they will need a number of different types of files. They may want an authored DVD. They may want a file for their website, mobile devices or broadcast. Always ask at the start of every project.

# 6

# GEAR

I have intentionally not provided a ton of information about gear. That's because the tools of the trade change much too quickly and it would make this book old before it was finished. With that said, I use a number of different traditional video cameras depending on the job but my Sony EX-1 is probably the camera that I choose most often for commercial or corporate shoots.

Because so many still photographers have embraced the DSLR as their "video" camera of choice, I have included a blog post that I had written before embarking on a trip around the world for the purpose of creating a feature length documentary. I opted to use a DSLR for this film because I wanted to shoot both still images and video and I knew that I could not bring two separate camera systems because we were limited to what would fit into two backpacks. The DSLR was the best tool (camera) for this project because it served both purposes.

### My DSLR Kit for a Three-Month Road Trip

If you have been following this blog then you know that I'm getting ready to depart for a 3-month trip around the world, creating a documentary with my daughter – *Opening Our Eyes*. Here is what I've managed to fit into two backpacks – it just fits. Thank goodness there's two of us.

Please follow our journey www.OpeningOurEyes.net

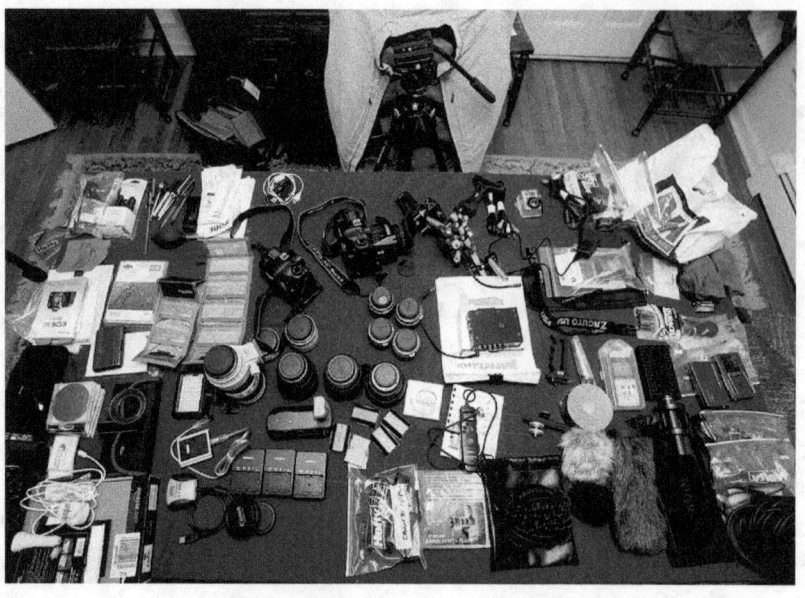

Canon 5D Mark II
Canon 7D
Canon 16-35mm 2.8
Canon 24-70mm 2.8
Canon 70-200mm 2.8
Canon 70-300mm 4.5
Canon 1.4X tele extender
Canon 2X tele extender
Nikon/Canon lens adaptor
Nikkor 14mm rectilinear lens f2.8
Nikkor 50mm 1.4
Nikkor 85mm f2
6 Batteries for Canon
1 Battery grip for 5D
3 Battery chargers
Remote control for Canon
AC adaptor for Canon
Rycote Hot shoe extension
4 – 16 GB flash cards – all cards – Sandisk UGMA
4 – 8 GB flash cards
2 – 8 GB SDHC cards
2 – 4 GB SDHD cards
Neutral density filter kit

Polarizer
Epson P6000 digital wallet
Zoom H4n digital audio recorder
JuicedLink DT454  audio preamp
Rode shotgun mic
Tram lav mic
Sennheiser Transmitter/Wireless kit
"Dead Cats" (windscreens)
XLR cords
Headphones
HD Hero helmet camera with attachments
Flip HD
ManfrottoTripod and fluid head
Small Matthews boom stand for mic
Reflector
Zacuto Z-Finder
Zacuto Striker Rig
Flex DSLR remote
Lacie Rugged Hard drives – 4000 GB memory!
Firewire and USB cords
3 – card readers
2 MacBookPro Laptops
1 extra laptop battery
1 extra AC adaptor for laptop
Kindle
iPod
2 Scotte Vests – with 22 pockets in each

# 7

# AUDIO IS MORE IMPORTANT THAN THE VIDEO

Audio is everything in video. I will repeat this because I can't stress this enough. Most times "capturing audio" is a skill that still photographers don't possess. I see a lot of confusion and misconceptions amongst still photographers as they move into video especially when using the DSLR camera. For many, audio is an after thought. Unless you know that you'll just be laying down still images or video clips to music, you will have to be able to capture good sound. If your job depends on good audio, my suggestion is to hire a good sound guy. The sure sign of an amateur is a video with bad audio.

**Here are some tips for getting good audio:**

- Don't use the camera's internal microphone except as a reference track.  If I'm shooting with a DSLR and recording my sound separately with a digital audio recorder I won't disable the camera's internal mic or turn the audio off even though I know I won't be using it. It comes in handy as a reference later on in post-production when I'm syncing the audio captured by the independent audio recorder with the video captured by the camera.

- Don't buy a camera that won't allow you to use external microphones unless you know that you will always be capturing your audio separately with a recording device and syncing it later in post.

- Never use "auto" when recording audio. Turn off the AGC (automatic gain control) on the DSLR cameras. Your audio will not be constant if you don't. If there are loud noises like coughs or clapping the auto feature will dial down your good audio as well as the bad.  You want to have control over your audio signal.

- Get your microphones in close. For b-roll situations you can probably get away with a shotgun microphone mounted on the camera. But microphones mounted on cameras can pick up camera noises. You can either use a microphone with a mini plug and connect it to the camera OR you can run the microphone via an XLR cord to a mixer like a JuicedLink or a Beachtek, which will give you better sound.

- When using a DSLR camera, capturing your audio separately with a separate digital recorder is ideal. I use a Samson H4N Zoom. It not only has built in dual stereo mics but two XLR inputs. I run my shotgun microphone and lav mic into the Zoom and then sync the sound later in post with software called Plural Eyes. Remember to keep the audio on in the camera because you will use it as a reference when syncing your sound with your visual.

- Use shotgun microphones for your interviews. Get them in close to your subject – no more than 1-3 feet away. I'm usually redundant when I set up microphones for interviews. I generally will use a shotgun microphone on a boom stand as well as a lav on my subject. This not only provides me with an audio backup in the event that I don't get clean audio from one of those sources, but I often will mix or blend the audio from those two sources in post. Lav microphones are usually more "bassy" especially with male subjects because they are positioned close to the throat. I like to mix that audio with audio captured from my shotgun mic that usually provides a fuller sound and picks up a bit of ambient audio or "nat sound" as well.

- Lav microphones attached to lapels can be hard wired or wireless. Be careful when positioning the lav to avoid any unnecessary noise from hair or jewelry rubbing against it.

- Go wired whenever possible. I only use a wireless system when I have no other choice. In cities like New York you can get a lot of interference on the frequencies. If you find yourself needing a wireless system then spend the money and get a system that has a good range.

- Use an omni-directional or cardiod microphone when you are in a more controlled environment and when you may want to capture sound coming from more than one direction. For example: If I am shooting an orchestra in a controlled environment like a sound stage or a performing arts venue that has great acoustics and I don't have to contend with ambient noise coming from an audience, then I will opt to use omni-directional microphones to capture sound coming from many different instruments as opposed to using shotgun mics that are more focused and will only pick up the audio coming from the instrument they are pointed at.

- Don't cross your audio cords with your electrical cords. This causes a hum that you will detect if you are wearing headphones. Make sure you use headphones and not just rely on audiometers. While the meters may indicate that you are capturing sound, you won't know if you are getting good clean sound. There could be hums or interference that you will only be able to detect if you are using headphones.

- Watch out for wind even indoors if the windows are open. Buy a good windscreen. Don't settle for the cheap foam wind screens that come with the microphone.

- Pay attention to audio. Start letting your ears do more of the work. Every room has its own sound. Listen. Turn off anything you can turn off like radios, TV's and fans. I even unplug refrigerators and I leave my car keys inside the fridge so that I can't leave the location without remembering to plug the fridge back in.

- Be quiet and tell your crew to be quiet as well. You never know when you'll want to use the audio. Even if you think you won't be using it, you may change your mind later.

- Always remember to capture "room tone". Every location and room has its own sound. The first thing I do when I get to a location is to ask everyone on set to be quiet and I listen to the sound of the room. Then I record 30 – 60 seconds of that room tone which I will use later in post to fill in the gaps between sound bites. Otherwise that soundless vacuum between audio gaps will stand out to your audience.

# 8

# GETTING GREAT INTERVIEWS

Getting a great interview is not only dependent on getting good audio but also dependent on your rapport with your subject. That's what will separate you from your competition, your ability to deliver the story through engaging interviews with your subjects.

**Some Interview Tips**

- Choose a suitable location. When looking for a location pick an environment that is not only appropriate for your subject but is a quiet environment that you will have control over. It's nice if the environment also provides more information about your subject.

- Ask your subjects to paraphrase the question. I don't insert myself into the piece I am creating. So, since the viewer will not be hearing my questions in the final video, I instruct my subjects to answer the questions in a manner that the viewer will have an understanding of what the question was even if they don't hear it. For example: If I ask my subject how many children they have, they shouldn't answer by saying "3". They should answer that question by saying "I have 3 children".

- Ask leading questions – not ones with yes and no answers. Don't ask the subject "Do you like where you work?" Ask them "What do you like about your work?" You don't want them to answer your question with a simple yes or no, but rather with an answer that provides more information. Stay away from questions that have yes or no answers.

- Don't step on your subjects' lines. Always allow a pause after your subject stops speaking before you ask the next question. In addition, instruct your subject to do the same and pause before they start answering your question. This will also allow your subject to collect their thoughts before answering the questions. This allows the editor breathing room as well as a clean place to cut the dialog without having overlapping voices making that a difficult task. I have also found that by pausing after my subject has answered a question, that many times they will add more meat to their answers and this usually yields more provocative thoughts.

- Be quiet and use non-audible gestures to affirm your subject's responses, rather than say things like uh huh, ok, hmmm etc.

- Be a good listener. Sometimes the best questions come out of listening to your subject. I always start out with my list of questions but sometimes my subject will say something that will provoke a really good question that I may not have thought of. If I'm not listening and merely referring to my notes and the next question I want to ask, I'll miss the gems. A good interviewer is a good listener.

- Remember to record room tone without anyone speaking. It's invaluable in post.

# 9

# BUILDING A TEAM AND COLLABORATION

Collaboration is essential in video production because there are so many facets and variables, each calling for different skill sets. Some collaborations occur simultaneously on set and some later in post-production but all players have to work together in order to get to the same end in harmony. Harmony means not just being able to get along but able to communicate and work together as a team. Collaboration works best when everyone on the team respects each other's role in the process.

It's very tricky to assemble the right mix of people but here are some important things to look for when building a team:

- **Trust** You have to be able to count on someone to do his or her job. Likewise, you need to commit and uphold your end of the deal. The team is only as good as the weakest link. That becomes even more critical the smaller the team is. If you're only working with one other person and you can't rely on them, you'll quickly find out that you'll end up doing most of the work yourself. It's important to know that the people you are working with are accountable and have your back.

- **Working Style** While it's not a necessity for everyone on the team to be "morning people" or "night people" or have identical working styles and habits, it can be extremely frustrating for all concerned if there are procrastinators on the team. That's because timing in video production is important for good workflow. If someone on the team doesn't deliver what he or she promised by the date they promised to deliver by it ultimately holds up the whole production. We had one situation where a motion graphics artist repeatedly missed his delivery deadlines. It held up the entire post-production process for months.

- **Expertise** Surround yourself with experts. They will make you look good. But remember, just because someone is expensive doesn't mean they are the best one for your job. There could be someone who is a better fit for the project who may be less expensive. Keep style and vision in mind. Talk to potential crewmembers and get reference

- **Right for the job** The "best" editor in terms of the commercial world might not be the right person for your project. For me, I want to work with an editor that is also *interested* in my project, in addition to how much it pays. I look for an editor who will bring a different perspective to the project as far as how the story gets told.

- **Bottom line** Work with people you can count on, otherwise the job might not get done.

**How do you build a motion/video production team? What resources are available for finding a production team — organizations, unions, agencies, directories?**

- To find producers as well as other crew check out the website of AICP (American Independent Commercial Producers) www.aicp.com/
- Another good place to find crew is www.shots.net
- Call ad agencies in your area to get recommendations for a good line producer. A good line producer will pull all the pieces together including putting together the right crew.
- Rental Houses. Ask the folks where you rent gear for crew recommendations. They usually have a pretty good pulse on the industry.
- Networking with your professional colleagues and attending things like Meet Ups and Final Cut User Group meetings or going to product demos and trade shows. In other words go to places where people who are working in various crew capacities hang out.
- Many cities and states have film commissions, which put out production guides and directories that have listings of people working in all sorts of crew capacities in their area.

## Video/Motion Crew

- **Producer** This person is essentially in charge of everything on the project, from the concept through the finances and scheduling of how and when things get done. For smaller projects the producer and director may be the same person who has a vision for how the end product will look and how the message or story will be delivered to the audience.

- **Director** The person who oversees all creative decisions on the project. They will direct the DP, the talent, and other members of the team including the editor. A director must exude confidence to instill trust amongst their crew as well as their client. They must be thought of and respected as the leader of the team.

- **Line Producer** The person who puts the crew together and handles all logistics of the shoot on site.

- **Director of photography (DP)** This is the person who is responsible for translating the concept from an idea to footage, taking care of lighting design, camera selection and pretty much anything else that involves capturing usable images. They may serve as their own camera operator or they may direct another camera operator to get the style and vision they are after.

- **Location sound recorder** On very small video productions the camera operator may cover this role but ideally you'll have one person who is responsible for nothing else other than making sure great sound is captured. Remember audio is everything in video production.

- **Editor** This is the person who takes all of the footage and sound captured during the shoot and whittles it down into a cohesive story that communicates the right ideas and emotions to the audience. They may be responsible for graphics, titles, music and the final "finishing" of the piece.

- **Writer** Critical for a good narrative.

**Other roles that may crop up depending on the needs of the project:**

- **Makeup/Hair** Same as in a still shoot. They're responsible for making sure the talent looks their best.

- **Wardrobe** Just as with hair and makeup this person is responsible for making sure the talent's wardrobe looks as good as possible as well as fits the tone and time period of the story that is being told.

- **Gaffer** They handle all lighting-related needs of the DP, from getting the right equipment to placing it in position and getting everything powered up.

- **Location manager** If you have a large number of locations needed this person will handle getting access, permits, location insurance, and scheduling. Basically their role is to make sure location needs and logistics are taken care of.

- **Sound editor** While the primary editor is concerned with the "picture", a sound editor is responsible for handling all sound-related editing for the project. This is usually necessary if a large amount of the sound is reliant on cutting together sound clips in post as opposed to using straight location sound.

- **Music supervisor** This person is responsible for supervising all music on the project. It may involve the selection music from sources that already exist or hiring a composer. They are also responsible for licensing all music and securing the necessary rights to the music.

- **Graphics artist** This person is responsible for providing whatever graphics the project may require. This would include the creation of simple text to complex animated motion graphics.

# 10

## STRUCTURING YOUR BUSINESS
## AND THE ROLE YOU SET FOR YOURSELF

The business of still photography changed forever when the "hybrid" camera came on the scene. Still imagery is just *one* medium that a visual creator needs to be proficient with in order to compete. In the last couple of years many still photographers have either closed shop or modified their business models to stay relevant with the changes in technology. Many still photographers are now offering video and motion services to their existing still photography clients. But many are also making mistakes from a business point of view and paying the consequences - going out of (the video business) before they've barely begun.

Many still photographers think that by buying a DSLR camera that also shoots video, that's all it takes to get into the video production business. The problem is they are thinking the same way they criticize their clients for when their clients hire a non-professional photographer to shoot their still needs because they can't discern the difference between a pro and an amateur. Still photographers who equate buying a still camera that has a "video mode" with being a professional motion shooter or videographer are forgetting some important factors.

- **Buying a DSLR is only a start.** Buying a DSLR that shoots video isn't all there is to getting into the business of video. In fact it might not even be the right tool for many video jobs. And if you do go the route of the DSLR keep in mind that most shooters spend sometimes *twice* as much as the price of these cameras on add-ons to make these cameras a viable tool for video production.

- **There are many facets to video production.** In fact positioning yourself as just a camera operator may not be the best business model. Still photographers are accustomed to ownership and holding the copyright to their work. Camera operators in the motion world are hired guns and turn over their footage with no stake in the copyright of the content they shoot.

  **There's a steep learning curve** in terms of the other aspects of video production namely, capturing good audio, editing, and output. Editing is a craft and working with a professional editor will raise the bar on the quality of your productions. While learning to edit and editing your own material will make you a better shooter, understand that it comes with a steep learning curve and a seasoned editor is well worth the money spent.

- **Video is a collaborative medium.** While I may be able to create a video from soup to nuts single handedly, I also know that the production will suffer if I try to do that. I know I can't be good at doing everything. I learned a long time ago to build a team made up of good sound people, editors and even camera operators that I can draw on to hire on a need be basis. They make the production and me look good and that's what keeps my clients coming back. It also allows my business to grow because I can take on more projects. If I'm not entrenched in all aspects of a production then it frees me up to start production on another project while still in post-production on a previous project. If you are a one-man band, you won't have this option and you may actually make yourself look *small* in the process.

  Video and motion have many facets to them. I advocate that the best business models are when one positions themselves at the top of the content creation ladder by overseeing the production of the whole and hiring the appropriate crew that will facilitate the process. By recognizing the differences between this business model and the "solo" model that most independent photographers work under you'll have a much better shot of maintaining ownership of your work and creative vision as well as having the potential to grow your business beyond your own singular capabilities.

- **Understand where the new opportunities are.** Don't try to compete in traditional markets like broadcast spots right away. Many new opportunities may be with your still photography clients who you already have a relationship with. They might also be new to motion and find themselves needing to produce a video. The clients you already have may be the first ones to approach in terms of marketing your new skills.

There are many different markets for video production and depending on which market you work in will depend on how you will structure your business. Commercial photographers working in advertising will most likely be working with large crews on big productions. They may choose to play the role of director or director of photography or they may want to position themselves as just camera operators. I work more journalistically with small crews in direct corporate and institutional markets.

Most times, I choose to assume the role of producer and take on the responsibility of the entire production. I usually direct as well as operate the camera. But we all know that it's not just about the gear and it's not a one size fits all when it comes to making choices in that regard. It's also not a one size fits all business when it comes to pricing in terms of usage and licensing. What might work in one market may not apply in another.

The point is that buying a DSLR isn't what will get you in the game of video production. There's more to it. And there isn't just a rack of template prices that apply to all. We are hired for who we are, how we see, how we work and our experience. The ones who will be successful will understand that it's not about just having a camera capable of shooting video.

# 11

## WORK FOR HIRE, COPYRIGHT AND LICENSING TALENT AND INSURANCE

Video is a collaborative effort that involves more parties than a typical still photographic project. It is customary especially in the traditional business models of film and TV broadcast that the copyright holder is the entity (company) that is producing the project. Rarely does the shooter hold copyright to what they create when working as part of the collaborative effort.

As I have previously mentioned, I position myself as the producer of most of the projects that I create. I try to maintain ownership and copyright of the "whole" piece. This works well when working with a client directly and taking responsibility for the whole production.

If you will be working solely as a DP or Camera Operator than most likely you will be working in a work for hire situation. If that's the case try to find value in other ways: Get more cash upfront or negotiate rights to use the piece as a portfolio sample.

### Work for Hire
- Depends on your business model – Are you the producer?
- Work must come within 1 of the 9 categories of work:
  - A contribution to a collective work
  - A part of a motion picture or audiovisual work
  - A translation
  - A supplementary work
  - A compilation
  - An instructional text
  - A test
  - Answer material for a test
  - An atlas
- The work must be specially ordered or commissioned.
- There must be a written agreement between the parties specifying that the work is a work made for hire.

### Copyright Tutorial
http://asmp.org/tutorials/copyright-overview.html

## Licensing

There are probably people who would argue with me as far as licensing being an acceptable practice in video production, other than the licensing of stock footage. Perhaps that may be true in some business models and certainly true in older business models, but I can tell you that has not been my experience.

I should clarify that I do not position myself as a "hired gun"– meaning a camera operator who turns over their footage at the end of the day. I choose to assume the role of producer and maintain control over my intellectual property or the finished video product. I cannot do this in the traditional motion picture industry but that business model is changing due to technology and the influx of Indie filmmakers who are making their own rules and bringing their films to market themselves. And for the most part, I can't do this in high-end broadcast spots when working with a middleman or ad agency where ultimately their end client maintains all rights. Generally speaking it's the one who pays for the production that owns the rights to the work. However, the demand for video has skyrocketed in recent years and with that a new breed of client has developed who is using video in new ways and on new platforms. I am establishing my own set of rules accordingly. One of them is licensing the finished product just as I do with my still images. I can only do that with video productions that I have produced and hold the copyright to.

Typically, I will separate the licensing of my still images from the video product as well as my creative fees. I may be shooting both mediums on the same job but I handle the licensing separately. I have found that video has a shorter shelf life so I am not as concerned about the duration of the license (length of time) as I am when I license still imagery. But I am concerned about its "reach" which these days is global thanks to YouTube. However, I am now able to upload videos that I create to YouTube or Vimeo and track the plays, downloads and embeds. This information can be very useful in showing the value of your work to your clients as well as provide them with information and stats that you can use when licensing your work.

Another thing I do is I make sure that it is clearly stated in my contracts and/or estimates that the license for the entire video production does NOT include permission and/or the license to use any "still images" that are made from frame grabs pulled out of the video footage. Putting this up front in the estimate has actually been very beneficial because if a client does anticipate the need for still images they will hire me to create stills rather than pull the stills from the footage.

We are living at a time where just about everyone's business model is changing. So if someone tells you that licensing video isn't the norm outside of the stock motion footage business, think again. What is the norm these days? We may be setting the precedent for the future.

## Licensing Music for Your Creations

Music is the heart of any film, TV show, broadcast spot or just about any other type of "content" that delivers a message. Personally, I think that music is of equal importance as the visuals, the dialog and the script, in setting the feel and pace for any of those "products" that I just mentioned. Imagine any of those entities without music!

While working on the post-production of a feature documentary I became aware just how important music was to the film and that I needed lots of it. In all I think we used over 53 pieces of music in a film that was 76 minutes long. And, I think we still could have used a little more in spots.

It's amazing to me how many professional photographers don't consider the licensing process when it comes to music. I've seen too many portfolio samples using "main stream" music that I know has not been licensed because it would have been prohibitively expensive. When you enter into the world of video production and begin incorporating music into your creative projects be prepared to spend some serious money and keep proper documentation. I learned a lot in this process and I'll share with you some tips:

- Make sure you have budgeted enough money for music especially if you are looking for broad rights. Even licensing royalty free music adds up if you need a mass-market license. That would include everything from TV to a theatrical screening to DVD's and VOD, internationally.

- Royalty free music comes with different tiers of licensing rights. One company I worked with www.neosounds.com has two options – Standard Licensing and Mass Market Licensing. The difference is that for TV broadcast a standard license is limited to national usage and a mass-market license grants you worldwide rights. So, anything that will go online will need a mass-market license because the world has access to it.

- Make sure you keep all licensing agreements as well as any receipts for the music you purchase both electronic and printed copies. You will need this documentation. If you want to mass duplicate DVD's you will be asked for proof of licensing.

- Keep track of the music, the title, the publisher, the recording company, the artist, and the songwriter as well as how much of the music was used (time) and where it is used in your film or video. You'll need all this information for your "cue sheet".

- A cue sheet is basically a list of all the music that is used in a film in the order that it appears with all the info I mentioned above listed. If a film festival accepts your film they will ask for it.

- Don't forget that most times you will need two licenses for a song. One is the "synchronization license" which grants you permission from the publisher to use the song and the other is the "master use license" which grants permission from the recording company for a particular recording of that song. Popular songs can be recorded hundreds of times by different artists.

- Apple Loops is "free" to use as long as you aren't reselling just those clips as clips. But you'll still need to download that license on the Apple website.

## Talent and Insurance Considerations When Switching to Video

Most still photographers make two critical mistakes when first venturing into motion:

**They are underinsured.** Video productions have more variables, larger crews and bigger budgets than still photography productions. While some insurance policies may be suitable for still photography shoots they will be inadequate if you get into larger video productions. Don't find out the hard way when your insurance company drops you or won't pay a claim when they find out that you are shooting video.

**Talent may belong to a union.** As soon as you flip into video mode on your DSLR you have entered into another realm as far as talent is concerned. Actors and actresses who belong to SAG (Screen Actors Guild) are bound to a very specific set of rules and pricing standards when they do video or motion shoots. You might have worked with the same models previously on your still photo shoots, but you will need to abide by certain rules when putting them in front of your motion camera.

I use a casting agent when I know I'll be using talent for a video shoot. A good casting agent will not only find the right people for your shoot, they'll take care of all the bookkeeping and other necessary paperwork. Find an agent that is savvy and is used to working with union talent.

Side note: Union rules may also apply to crew if you are working with union crew.

# 12

# POST PRODUCTION AND EDITING

• Determine if you will edit the project yourself. Editing has a steep learning curve but even knowing a little or sitting in on an editing session with your editor will make you a better shooter. You will know as soon as you start to edit what shots you should have gotten during the production part of the process. One thing becomes quite clear in the editing room and that is you can never seem to shoot enough b-roll.

• Leave the editing to the pros if you have the budget. It's a craft in itself and a professional editor will give polish to your piece.

• Video editing is an ongoing process with your client unlike still photography where you deliver the files and the job is done. With editing there are various rounds of approval. Many times I deliver the best sound bites from the interviews to my client and wait for their approval before adding the other elements like b-roll, music, titles etc.

• Good workflow is critical. I do double and triple backups of everything in the field. I keep separate folders for Interviews (A-Roll), B-roll, still images, music, audio files, motion graphics etc.

• I gather all my assets before I begin to edit. That includes any stock images, footage, music, logos or anything else that will need to be integrated into the final piece.

• I avoid jump cuts. When editing interviews you will be "cutting" out all the unwanted remarks, ums, and restarts of sentences of your subjects. When you start cutting these unwanted segments from your subject interviews and begin moving parts of the interview around, your subjects no doubt will have moved because people don't remain absolutely stationary. Therefore the head placement of your subject will appear to shift where the cuts have been made causing the image to "jump". B-roll is used to cover these edits.

- Cut on the action to make the edits seamless and not draw attention to them. For example cut from a wide shot of someone putting a key in the ignition of a car to a close-up of the key being turned in the ignition.

- Avoid cheesy transitions like dissolves.

- Let the piece breathe by pacing the interviews with b-roll, still imagery and music in between.

- Use music to create a feeling. It can be very effective when using an underscore of music with an interview as long as the viewer can still hear and understand the dialog.

- Step back every now and then to make sure you are telling the story that you want to tell. Ask a neighbor or a friend to look at your piece and ask them what they think the story is about. If they are unclear or confused then you know you have more work to do.

- Be prepared to make a variety of files for DVD, web and mobile devices. This can be a profit center.

- Cut down on how many times and how long a "talking head" stays on the screen. Use more b-roll to cover up the talking head visual while the dialog continues underneath. It adds more interest. A good rule of thumb is 80% B-roll and 20% talking head.

- Break up sections of interviews with interesting image sequences to music. It lets the piece breathe.

- Don't make cuts in your b-roll in the middle of a word. Always cut between the words of your subjects' dialog.

- Choose your fonts carefully for text. Sans serif fonts work best and try to keep it simple and in keeping with the story. Make sure your text stays on the screen long enough for your viewer to read it - around 6 seconds for lower thirds and titles.

- Never start a piece with text or titles. Always start with your best images to grab a viewer's attention.

## Licensing other work

Most photographers are accustomed to licensing their images but not familiar with negotiating and licensing other people's work whether it is negotiating rights for stock images, footage or music. It's important to remember that not everything is for sale, especially mainstream music. Don't make the mistake of using a popular song as a placeholder and then having to tell your client it isn't available for any amount of money.

When you license music, you must remember that you need to license the recording rights as well as the publishing rights. Sometimes it's the same person who writes the song and sings it, but sometimes it's not. Regardless, those rights are licensed separately.

With any licensing you must consider the territory (where it will be seen or heard), the term (for how long), the medium (for the web, in a movie, on TV) and if you are asking for exclusive rights. If your budget allows it work with a music rights clearance agent. It can be extremely time consuming.

# 13

# BREAKING DOWN VIDEO PRODUCTION

There are a lot more variables in video production than there are in still photography. That means more responsibility and more things to think about. Even for the simplest video productions you will need to think things through from the story planning to the deliverables.

## Proposal/Estimating

When you work on an estimate for a job the first thing you should figure out is what you will outsource and what you will do in house. You will also need to know your cost of doing business to be able determine how much you should charge in the way of your fees in order to make a profit. To determine your cost of doing business you need to add up all your costs (including your overhead costs) and figure out how much you need to make each day to stay in the black.

There are professionals out there who specialize in drawing up proposals and estimates. If you have been asked to estimate on a video production project and you are new to video production, I would highly suggest you hire a producer who has experience. They will know what will be needed to execute the job and the costs involved. They will also be knowledgeable in crew resources and be able to pull the pieces of the job together if you should be fortunate enough to get it.

When working on estimates I will need to find out all the details that will be required to complete the job. I also need to know the client's priorities. Do they want it fast, good or cheap – or all three? I tell them to pick two.

## Pre-Production

Pre-production will include initial meetings with the client.
Storyboard, script approval and schedule of deliverables with sign-offs.
Assembling a crew and determining how many cameras and other gear needed.
Scouting and picking locations.
Casting Talent.
Travel arrangements.
Scheduling and drawing up call sheets. (who is supposed to be where and when)

## Production - the shoot
This includes everything and anything on the shoot
Crew
Talent
Catering
Transportation needs

## Post-Production
Researching and outsourcing additional needs – stock footage, still images, graphics and music
Working with voiceover talent to create the narrative.
Editing or working with an editor.
Working with a motion graphics person.
Working with a music composer.
Working with an audio engineer for the final mix.

## Facilitation/Delivery
This includes making sure all the deliverables are met.
DVD's and BluRays
Files for VOD and online – H.264, mp4, mpeg 2, flv, avi etc.
Fulfillment of hard deliverables and packaging, including working with a graphic designer to produce artwork for the packaging.


**The most important thing is to determine who will be responsible for what and when. If you're the producer you will be ultimately responsible for everything and everyone involved.**

# 14

# ESTIMATING AND THE QUOTE

Pricing by the minute is ludicrous. You could be commissioned to do one locked down shot for a one-minute final piece or 500 short clips using specialized gear that will also be edited to a one-minute final product. Price by the usage and the market value.

I will estimate a job based on the assumption that I may be outsourcing everything – the shoot, the sound, the editing and the deliverables. This allows me to choose which roles I want to keep in house, and make the revenue accordingly. That way if another project comes along it will allow me to take it on without going into the red on the previous job if we have to absorb the costs of outsourced services that weren't taken into consideration in the budget of our initial estimate.

There are lots of production houses and camera operators that put their rate sheets on their websites. These can be handy to use as a quick reference as far as what your competition charges. I don't publish my rate sheet online but I do use it for internal purposes. I determine the "rates" and "creative fees" that I need to charge by calculating my cost of doing business.

I will also reference past jobs and time logs kept from past editing projects. I use the Association of Independent Producers Form, which has itemized categories so that I don't inadvertently leave something out. I do not line item my production costs on my estimates. I don't want a potential client to determine what I should cut out of my budget. If the budget does need to be trimmed, it will allow me to address which areas I feel I can cut without compromising the job.

Most importantly, I need to figure out the scope of the job and this means asking the client a lot of questions. I will first try to get a sense of their budget. Many times a client won't tell you their budget but you can always ask "Is it less than…" to try and get a basic idea of what they have to spend. You don't want to waste your time working on an estimate for a job that you think is a $50,000 job only to find out that their budget is less than $10,000.

## The Questions:

- **Who** is the end client?
- **What** are the specifics of job – specialized gear, talent, voiceover talent, locations, script writing, storyboard, stock footage needs, and motion graphics needs, music, deliverables? What are the expectations or goals?
- **When** is the deadline for the job to be finished?
- **Where** will it been seen? Who is the audience?
- **How** will the job be executed? What is the approach? Are they looking for humor, a testimonial style, lots of motion graphics?

Here is a list of some of the questions we asked a client in order for us to properly estimate a job. The job was to produce 3 (less than 5 min.) videos for a new technology that a company had invented and wanted to license. They were using the video to recruit potential investors:

- Will each video have a separate script and or Voiceover track? Who will write the script?
- Who will create the storyboard? (Includes narrative and description of interview sound bites and b-roll footage.)
- Who will research voiceover talent and direct the talent for the voiceover?
- What are the talent needs? Who will handle the casting and pay for the talent?
- What sorts of locations are needed? Will there be travel?
- Will there be logos or any other graphics that need to be created, 3D graphics or computer generated motion graphics?
- Who will research the graphics needed?
- Will there be any stock photo or footage needed? Who will do the research and whose budget will the stock costs come out of?
- Music – will it be original and commissioned for the project? Who will handle that hire and direction?
- What format will the job be shot in – HD? Will it be staged? Will we have control over the action? Will it be an event type scenario with no control over the action?
- What are the final output files? Example: DVD's? Who will handle the artwork for packaging? Who will take care of the duplication?
- What other files are needed? Example: Web Video files - H.264, FLV, WMV, mp4 – what types of files are needed? What are the dimensions of the files – 1280 pixels x 720 pixels?
- For web videos – who will host the video? Whose server will it reside on? Who will upload the file to the server?

After I feel that I have sufficient information to present an estimate I will present the estimate as clearly and simply as possible.

**Approach:** This will be a description of the details of the job as well as how we will approach the job. This will include the size of the crew, the stylistic approach, what is included in the estimate as well as what isn't included. I will also provide a rough timeframe for completion.

**Creative Fee:** I will line item my creative fees. If I am asked to shoot still images, as well I will line item that creative fee separately.

**Usage and Licensing:** I will detail licensing rights and usage if applicable.

**Expenses:** I will usually provide a range for expenses but won't break them out. A bid is different than an estimate in that it usually mandates that you stay within a 10% variance.

**Terms:** Here is where I will list payment terms as well as the liabilities and responsibilities of both parties. I may also include a sign off schedule for workflow as well as details concerning any changes.

# 15

# The S.O.W. (STATEMENT OF WORK)

Once you get the job you'll want to initiate an S.O.W. (Statement of Work) between your client and yourself. It is just as important in this statement of work to articulate not only what the job includes, but also what it doesn't include. All terms should be clearly spelled out, including terms of payment as well as any licensing and usage rights granted.

I try to keep my contracts simple, yet at the same time leave no stone unturned. Invariably, many of the terms that I have added over the years have been the result of learning the hard way.

**Key elements of our S.O.W.'s include:**

- A cover sheet that explains how we will approach the job creatively, what type of gear we'll be using and why, the crew and locations needed and why our team is best suited for this project.
- Our creative fees. We list our still photography creative fee separate from our video creative fee.
- Production costs. We don't line item everything but we do break out expenses. i.e.: production costs, post-production etc. We have found that in the past when we line item expenses, including crewmember costs individually, some clients have taken it upon themselves to eliminate some crew needs that may be critical to doing the job professionally.
- Terms. State payment terms, usually 40% upon acceptance of the job, 40% upon delivery of the rough cut and the balance upon delivery of the final cut.
- Copyright, licensing and usage terms. State who holds the copyright for both for the still photos and the video footage and any licensing or usage fees and terms. We always license our still images separately from our video footage.
- State clearly what is included in the price and what isn't included.
- Change orders. What constitutes a change order and how that impacts the final budget?
- Include a clause stating that video footage cannot be used as still images. (frame grabs)
- Timeline for project with benchmark dates and sign-offs by client.

Here is an example of a very simple S.O.W. – This was the follow up to an estimate that had been previously approved.

## STATEMENT OF WORK

### PROJECT
Kelly/Mooney will produce five 3-5 minute videos, output for both DVD and web, which display, explain and compare the application of Ice Engineering's compelling disruptive engineering science to ice interface technologies for executive business leadership in the following target markets:

1. Automotive
2. Ice making (consumer and commercial)
3. Industrial refrigeration
4. Residential refrigeration
5. Power lines

### Project Includes:
Pre-production meetings
Storyboard to illustrate provided script
Casting – talent and voiceover talent
Three day - video shoot on location at Dartmouth, New Hampshire – to include interviews and b-roll
Expenses on location
Researching stock photography and stock footage
Post production - edit of 5 videos – not to exceed 5 minutes each and export to DVD and web files (2 file types per video) – Includes delivery of rough cut, one revision and final edit

### Project does NOT include:
Still Photography
Stock photography or video footage licensing costs
Talent and/or voiceover talent
Motion graphics
Script
Specialized gear – helicopters, gyros, cranes etc.
Archiving
Additional crewmembers not mentioned above.

### Licensing Rights:
Rights for internal and external corporate and PR usage for 3 years.  No broadcast rights or paid advertising.
No rights granted for still images derived from frame grabs from video footage.

---

**TOTAL PRODUCTION COST\*:$XX,XXX – $XX,XXX** based on details to date. *Subject to revision.

**PAYMENT TERMS:**

1ST PAYMENT DUE NOW
**$XX,XXX**  40% of Total project costs.

2ND PAYMENT DUE 8/27
**$XX.XXX**  40% of Total project costs

<u>FINAL PAYMENT DUE UPON DELIVERY OF FINAL CUTS</u>
**$XX,XXX** Balance due.

_____

**$XX,XXX Total**

\*Cancellation prior to 8/14 - client is liable for pre-production fees and any expenditure to date
\*Cancellation after 8/14 - client is liable for pre-production, 50% of crew fees and any expenditure to date.
\*Cancellation after 8/19 - client is liable for pre-production, 100% crew, 50% shoot fees, expenditure to date.

---

**WORKING TIMELINE:**

| | |
|---|---|
| 7/29 | Conceptual treatments (one-pager's) |
| 8/05 | Working script drafts – deliver needs for storyboard creation |
| 8/12 | Script breakdown or simple storyboard drafts |
| 8/12 | Graphics & animation simple storyboard drafts |
| 8/20 | Final production scripts |
| 8/24 - 8/28 | Location filming, graphics and animation creation |
| 9/4 | Deliver graphics and voiceover track to editor |
| 9/18 | Rough edits |
| 9/30 | Final edits |

**CHANGES:** Any changes or additions deemed as significant from the agreed upon scope (limitations) of the project's work requires a mutual agreement and will require additional fees and an additional Statement of Work.

**\*Please sign this agreement and return via fax at 973/543-9594.**

**Thank you.**

_____ Sign          _____ Date

_____ Name

# 16

# COMMISIONED vs. SELF-INITIATED PROJECTS

Notice I didn't say "personal projects". That's because a "personal project" sounds like it has no monetary value. The phrase "self-initiated project" somehow conveys a different idea. In the entertainment industry "self-initiated projects" are done all the time and at very high levels, with "name" actors producing and directing their own films where they call the shots and hopefully reap the rewards of their efforts.

Photography and video, in and of themselves are not *business models*, but rather they are mediums that are used commercially, non-commercially and personally. The business aspect of photography and video comes into play when you determine how you will apply these mediums in order to sustain a business in terms of today's markets.

Today's markets are global. That's good news and bad news depending on the type of work you do. If you are a stock photographer or even if you have expanded into also shooting stock motion footage, your inventory or your content must be unique in some way in order to sustain that type of business model in our global economy. You will need to stand out if you pursue this market.

If you are a commissioned commercial or editorial photographer, a cinematographer, or a director, the competition is fierce and once again if you don't have a unique style or vision, most likely you will end up playing by other people's rules or signing "their" contracts. It comes down to supply and demand of talent and work and you will either need to compete on price or by offering something that you can do better than your competition.

The good news is if you are willing to do the work, the world is your stage. The portals for distribution of your "content" are open to all and as creators we are no longer dependent on the middleman. When I get asked to talk about "new business models" I always look at it by asking myself "Where are the new opportunities?" Where can I carve out my own "new business model" rather than adapt to other people's ideas of what that may be.

There is a big difference in these two approaches. I am carving out a business model for who I am creatively and where I see the most opportunities for what I do well. When I am authentic to who I am and apply this to my work, I am able to get the type of work to market that I do best and reach the right audience while maintaining ownership and control over the licensing of my work. I am able to do that not only because technology has enabled me, but more importantly it there is a demand for the type of content that I create.

Think about it. What are your strengths? What are your passions? Now imagine a business model based on your answers. The world is our stage.

These days, because of the ease with which we can of connect and communicate with one another globally, we as individual creators are empowered by our ability to reach a much wider audience. But there is one thing that I have learned first hand by working on my own film project and that is – It's a LOT of WORK. That's because you will find yourself playing a lot of roles. In my case, I was producing the film, directing it, shooting it and doing the grunt work on the post-production. And just when I thought my movie was finished, I realized the real work had just begun to promote and market it.

For me, promotion and marketing is the worst part of the process. I'd much rather spend my time creating. But what's the point of making a movie if no one ever sees it? So you either have to do the promotion and marketing yourself or pay someone to do it. That's where the *business* part kicks in. But if you follow through and do the work, the possibilities are endless and the rewards can be many.

The bottom line is you need to decide for yourself - what works best for the type of person you are? If you are a big picture person with a tolerance for risk and not averse to working long hours, then "self-initiated" projects may be the way to go. But it's not for everyone and certainly not for the faint hearted.

# 17

# CROWD FUNDING, SOCIAL MEDIA AND BUILDING AN AUDIENCE

## Building Your Audience

The most important item mentioned in the title of this chapter is "building an audience". That's because without an audience your crowd funding campaigns will fail and you'll be talking to yourself on social media platforms.

I had been writing a blog, *Journeys of a Hybrid* for a few years, when I came up with an idea for a film project. My "following" was comprised mostly of still photographers who were interested in pursuing motion. When I decided to make my film project a reality and announce it to the universe the first thing I did was to create another blog for the project, called *Opening Our Eyes*. I started the process of building an audience for the film (before it was even made) by writing the following post on my "journeys" blog:

*"I am embarking on a self-initiated project called Opening Our Eyes. The idea behind the project is to make a documentary that features people who are making a difference around the world – people who have followed their dreams, passions and ambitions and started their own personal "causes" that help make the world a better place, essentially a film about ordinary people who are doing extraordinary things.*

*In looking for people or subjects for my documentary I want to utilize the power of social media and reach out to my connections and friends, not only to find these folks, but also to make this project an interactive experience from the start. So, two days ago I launched a simple website and blog and gave the idea a name, "Opening Our Eyes – Global Stories About the Power of One".*

*My daughter Erin is teaming up with me on this project. She lives in Chicago – I live in NJ – but with social media we can bridge that divide as well as get the involvement of our separate networks of "friends". I was able to set up a simple blog and website and get it online in less than a day. The site will grow as we both continue to add content and relevant links and information, but by getting the idea "out there" and providing a way for feedback and dialog to take place, we are building our own community at the same time.*

*After the site was created, I created a fan page on Facebook with information about the project and links to the website. I also registered the blog with Network Blogs and inserted a "follow this blog" button on the fan page. Then I tweeted about project on Twitter, which automatically shows up on my own personal Facebook page. I also sent out about 50 emails to people I know.*

*The response has been overwhelming. Within a day I have received over 50 ideas about people and their causes. We've had well over 300 hits on the site and almost 40 fans have liked us on Facebook. Now that might not seem like a lot to some people, but to us it was an amazing response in such a short time period. As the project takes shape fueled by the interest and eagerness of our participants we are building a community and opening others' eyes to the "power of one"."*

I didn't realize it at the time but what I was doing was engaging and building an audience for our film. This ended up being critical to our success with our crowd funding campaigns as well as creating an audience who eagerly awaited the completion of the film. We attracted mothers and daughters who followed us vicariously throughout our travels as well as my professional peers who were interested in how I actually was "making" the movie. Our audience was building and growing virally as I continued to maintain two blogs.

## Social Media

I also worked other aspects of social media with a Facebook Fan Page for the film, my personal FB page, two twitter accounts (one for the film), LinkedIn, as well as uploaded videos on YouTube and Vimeo. There have been countless hours spent on various social media platforms over the last couple of years and I can honestly say that it was time well spent because I have applied it to a purpose, which in my case was making people aware of a documentary that I was creating.

The downside of social media is that you run the risk of over doing it by annoying people. There's a balance. Some say your posts should be 80/20 - meaning 80% of your posts should be sharing information and 20% or less should be about self-promotion. I have seen a shift in these social media platforms over the last couple of years as more and more people use them heavily as promotional tools.

## Some do's and don't tips for social media:

- Be consistent and strategic with your "brand". Create a plan. Who are you? What do you have to say?
- Listen first – then engage in the conversation.
- Build your community. Who will you follow? Who do you want to attract?
- Be authentic and share – provide value and relevant, useful content.
- Don't sell.
- Use links and provide news.
- Create and sort your groups on Facebook. Separate personal and business "friends".

• Set up a Facebook Fan Page for your business and complete the profile, including a photo.
• Take part in discussions on Linkedin.
• Set up an editorial calendar for your blog. This will give you a structure.
• Make comments on other blogs. Become an expert.
• Use tools like Hootsuite to organize and automate tweets.
• Don't create tweets with more than 120 characters. Leave room for re-tweets.
• Use www.search.twitter.com for topics and people.
• Set up "alerts" with Google so you will be notified when and where your name is mentioned
• Use @(name) in your tweets when you mention someone who doesn't follow you.
• Set up a daily routine. This will help with time management.

## Crowd Funding

Here are some things that I have learned through the process of getting our film funded on Kickstarter.

- *You* have to do the work. Once you launch your project page on Kickstarter, you need to let potential backers know about it using social media, email blasts or word of mouth. Just like getting traffic to your website, you can't expect people to stumble upon your project and fund it.

- *You* have to make it fun. Have fun with the "rewards" that you offer your backers, and on Kickstarter every project must have rewards. People love to give, but they also love to feel like they are part of something or that they have helped to make something happen. If a backer contributed to my project at the $500 reward level they received an Associate Producer credit in the film and on the project's website, along with DVD's of the film when it was completed, as well as a signed print and an e-book about the project's journey.

- Keep your financial goal realistic. Look at other projects that are similar to yours and see what the "market will bear". See what has been successful and ask yourself why. Remember that if you ask for too much money and you don't meet 100% of your goal by the time the funding period is over for your project, you won't receive anything. Only projects that are successfully funded at 100% will receive funds.

- Use social media and email blasts with common sense but don't be obnoxious. If you do send emails, don't send an email again to someone who has already backed your project. Ask people to share your project link on social media but don't overdo it.

- Post updates on your project to keep your backers and potential backers informed. Use visuals if you have them, both on your page site as well as in your updates. Photographs and videos really give a project presence and are a must have. You want to stand out from the crowd.

- There is no such thing as a pledge too small. They say the average pledge on Kickstarter is around $25 and I can attest to that. Out of our 161 backers, 69 had made pledges of $25. It all adds up. And every time someone backs your project there is also the opportunity that they may share it with someone they know who may in turn make a contribution.

- Be grateful and appreciative. I made it a point to send each and every one of my backers a personal thank you note.

- Have faith, because anything is truly possible these days.

# 19

# Film Festivals

Just like everything else, things have changed in terms of what a film festival can do for a film. It used to be that a festival could up your film's chances of getting picked up for distribution, but these days that usually only happens at the top tier festivals like Sundance or Cannes. And getting into top tier festivals is like winning the lottery – it's highly competitive.

However there are advantages to getting your film into festivals. It builds credibility for your film especially if you are fortunate enough to win an award. When I started speaking to distributors they all wanted to know the film's "festival track record". This may be more important for a narrative film than for a documentary, which has more of an afterlife outside the four walls of a theater, but nevertheless it can help get a buyer's or distributor's attention.

Another big advantage of having a film in a festival is it provides opportunities to network with other filmmakers and people in the filmmaking business. Obviously that's only an advantage if you attend the festivals and that requires more money to be spent. But what's the point of having a film in a festival if you don't attend your screening and interact with the audience? Some filmmakers go all out at festivals bringing in their entire cast and hosting a party or a special event to attract the attention of the press and potential distributors. Some festivals are more niche festivals focused around films with specific themes like "social issues". This allows filmmakers to network with like-minded people outside the creative community who are a more targeted audience.

In order to maximize the benefits that a festival can bring to a film it's important to remember a few things:

- **Have a strategy.** If you plan to submit to the top tier festivals, then be aware that some of these festivals want films to premiere at their festival. This means you will need to be strategic as far as which festivals to apply to and the order in which you do it. Once your film has premiered it may make it ineligible for another festival. If you have a film that has never been seen before, that could be a plus. Read all the rules carefully so that you don't inadvertently make your film ineligible for one festival by being in another.

- **Use Withoutabox.** You can upload all of the information that you will need to submit to most film festivals one time and in one place on Withoutabox. You can even upload a trailer and a full screener. Withoutabox allows you to submit your film to hundreds of film festivals and pay your entry fees directly from their website. It's a great time saver if you think you will be entering a lot of festivals.

- **Plan a budget for film festival expenses.** You'll need to produce all kinds of promotional materials if you get invited to a festival, everything from posters to postcards and that takes money. You will also need to budget for travel expenses. If you do get into a festival ask for help with travel expenses. Many times a festival will give you a bit of money toward your travel costs or be able to provide accommodations. If they don't offer, always ask.

- **Start preparing collateral for festivals before you are accepted.** Once you get into a festival you need to get into overdrive mode, gathering and sending all the things that a festival will request: exhibition screeners, screeners for press, posters, postcards, photos and press releases. Anticipate that you *will* get into a festival and start getting prepared ahead of time because they don't usually give you a lot of notice.

- **Don't rely on the festival to promote your screening.** You've got to promote your film yourself. Many festivals subscribe to platforms like "festival genius" that will help you promote your film. Take advantage of this or a festival's Facebook Fan page or Twitter account to create a "buzz". Utilize the festival's press office if they have one. They can give you a list of local media and you can send out press releases for your film. We did that for one festival and we wound up being interviewed on a local talk radio station.

- **Recognize this opportunity for finding your niche audience.** Go to your screenings and get feedback from your audience. If an audience member makes a great comment about your film, write it down and ask them if you can use it as a testimonial. Testimonials are great additions to press kits. Get email addresses from your audience and plan to sell DVD's at the festival unless you have signed a distribution deal that prohibits that. I always brought a stack of DVD's and a clipboard for gathering email addresses to every screening. Selling DVD's helped me tremendously by paying for some of my travel expenses.

- **Network** with other filmmakers and folks involved with the festival. There are always plenty of parties and other events that provide great opportunities for networking. Make sure you get people's cards. I usually make a note on the cards that I collect so that I remember something about the person who gave me the card. Example: "John knows educational distributors. Follow up and send a screener to him".

- **Publicize your festival acceptances and wins.** Promote the fact that your film has been accepted by a festival or has won an award. Good press about your achievements creates a buzz for the film and opens up future possibilities for your film after you have finished submitting to festivals.

# 20

# MONETIZATION OF SELF-INITIATED PROJECTS AND DISTRIBUTION

I don't define the word "photographer" by the type of camera he or she shoots with. Whether someone is shooting with a still camera, a traditional video camera, a motion picture film camera or a hybrid camera that shoots both stills and video, a "photographer" these days is apt to embrace more than one medium.

Regardless of the tools you may be using, I've come up with a few tips on how photographers can make money in this changing economy.

- **You don't need someone else to commission your services in order for you to make a living.** When photographers take on self-initiated projects not only are they creating a buzz and getting noticed by potential clients, they are also creating their own "content" that they can monetize. It is possible these days to get our content to market without the need of a middleman. Distribution portals are open to all.

- **Take advantage of what is "free" rather than be put out of business by it.** There are so many ways to build your brand and get noticed without spending a fortune. The costs of building and maintaining a website have dropped significantly because of advances in technology. Utilizing social media platforms to create a buzz and get the word out about your company is virtually free with Facebook, Twitter, LinkedIn and YouTube. But be prepared to do the work and discipline yourself because this territory is ripe with distractions.

- **Re-purpose your content.** If you've been blogging or have something useful to share consider packaging your "knowledge" into ePubs, podcasts or "how to" webinars. One thing I've learned about making an ePub is that you can either do it yourself or hire a formatter so that it gets to market quickly via Amazon, Barnes and Noble or the iTunes platform. Price it right and offer more than one ePub at a time.

If someone has just spent $3 or $4 to buy your ePub and they see you have another one for sale it's not a big stretch for them to buy that additional book if you have one to offer at the same time.

- **Re-purpose your "perks" from crowd funding campaigns.** If you've done any crowd funding campaigns like Kickstarter or IndieGoGo, then you've more than likely had to create perks to offer backers. Things like DVD's, prints and postcards or even items like stainless steel water bottles or reusable grocery totes with your brand's logo on them can make nice perks that are relevant to your project. You can monetize these items after your project has been funded and completed. This will also help push your brand out in the marketplace at the same time.

- **Collaborate with others.** Partner with others to put on webinars, podcasts, call in phone seminars etc. Use this opportunity to build your own brand. Don't always feel that you have to be the only "act" offered. In fact many times, if you join forces with other creatives, it will get you further than if you are the only speaker in a half filled room. Get out there and get noticed and learn from your colleagues at the same time.

- **Be patient.** Everything turns around. While the old days and ways of doing things won't come back, better opportunities will replace them. Don't be paralyzed by your own fears. Do what you can that won't cost you a lot of money and there is plenty you can do. Work social media, learn new skills – audio, editing, writing etc. Network with people, create new content for ePubs, webinars, and podcasts. Use your imagination and pursue what you are passionate about.

# Distribution

The goal of any filmmaker, photographer or writer is to get their work published or distributed. In distribution there are a lot of "catch-22's". You can't get an acquisitions director or publisher to take a look at your film or book because they will only talk to a literary or sales agent. But you can't get an agent unless you've had something published or distributed. And let's not forget that if you do negotiate a deal through a sales agent, the agent will also get a cut.

## Types of Distribution
Domestic - DVD, VOD and broadcast
Foreign - DVD,VOD and broadcast
Self-distribute - DVD and VOD

Theses days, there are alternatives to getting an sales agent and going the traditional route and that is to go directly to a distributor or self-distribute your film through portals like Amazon, iTunes or an aggregator like Distribber who you pay to get your content uploaded to these portals. But they don't do the promotion and marketing for your film. You will need to take care of that by yourself or hire someone to do it for you.

Filmmaker and author Jon Reiss coined the phrase "PMD" or Producer of Marketing and Distribution. Reiss stresses how important it is to allocate half of a film's budget and time to its promotion and marketing. To do that properly, one needs to dedicate a member of the team for that purpose and to get them involved early on in the process of making the film. This person's job is to find and engage "the audience" for the film. This could mean engaging a potential audience via social media platforms, submitting to film festivals, setting up community screenings or finding distribution outlets for the film.

One option for distribution of your film is to join a cooperative like New Day Films. If you apply and are accepted into this co-op, your film will become part of their catalog of films that are licensed to various educational and institutional outlets. The filmmakers need to pay for the DVD runs as well as all promotional material and efforts, but New Day handles the fulfillment. Each member filmmaker is also expected to attend an annual meeting and do some volunteer service but the filmmakers keep a much larger percentage of the profits.

## Self-Distribution
Distribber - aggregator
Film DIY - streams your film for rentals or sales
Topspin - Online marketing and sales portal
VHX - distribute direct online

## Educational Distribution
New Day Films
Bullfrog Films
Documentary Educational Resources

## International Distributors
Films Transit International – Canada
Cats & Docs – France
Autlook Films – Austria
HanWay Films – UK

## Distributors -US
New Video Films
First Run Features
Icarus Films
IndiePix Films

# 21

# WORDS OF WISDOM

I'd like to pass along the best advice I ever got.  In the early days of my career, after graduating from Brooks Institute of Photography, I was working as an assistant to a commercial "studio" photographer who shot food and product photography. My heart had always been in photojournalism and travel photography ever since traversing the globe prior to attending Brooks.  But at that period in time the markets for magazine publishing and photojournalism were changing and everyone was telling me that to make a viable living as a photographer I had to focus my efforts on commercial and advertising work. I listened and created a portfolio of images with those commercial markets in mind.

I had been fortunate enough to get an appointment with the legendary commercial photographer Jay Maisel who agreed to talk to me and look at my portfolio. I proudly showed him my perfectly executed commercial work and he took one look at my portfolio and told me that it was "garbage".  He asked me if this was what I wanted to do and that he didn't think my heart was in it. I told him that my heart was in journalism but that everyone was advising me to pursue another path.  He then asked me how old I was.  I replied "25 year old".  He looked me straight in the face and said, "You're 25 years old and you're already making compromises?"

That day was a turning point in my life.  I made a commitment to always listen to my heart and the voice inside me and trust that they would never guide me wrong.  I've had lots of misses and rejections along the way pursuing things that I thought I wanted at the time, but looking back I can see that these were all lessons that I needed to learn.  Even though I am now more than twice the age I was when I met with Maisel, I can still hear his words of advice running through my head whenever I begin to think about making compromises in my life and in my career.

I pass this advice along to you.

9 781482 544268